DATE DUE

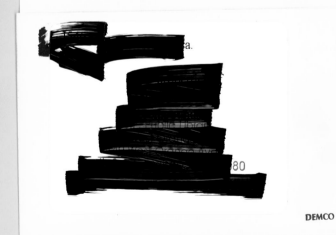

DEMCO

The Properties of
Elements and
Compounds

Lisa Hill

Chicago, Illinois

Editorial: Megan Cotugno, Andrew Farrow, and Clare Lewis
Design: Philippa Jenkins
Illustrations: KJA-artists.com
Picture Research: Ruth Blair
Production: Alison Parsons
Originated by Modern Age
Printed and bound in China by Leo Paper Group

13 12 11 10 09
10 9 8 7 6 5 4 3 2 1

Library of Congress Cataloging-in-Publication Data
Hill, Lisa.
 The properties of elements and compounds / Lisa Hill. -- 1st ed.
   p. cm. -- (Sci-hi. Physical science)
 Includes bibliographical references and index.
 ISBN 978-1-4109-3245-7 (hc) -- ISBN 978-1-4109-3260-0 (pb) 1. Chemical elements. 2. Inorganic compounds. 3. Chemistry, Organic. I. Title.
 QD466.H55 2008
 546--dc22
                       2008027375

Acknowledgments
The author and publishers are grateful to the following for permission to reproduce copyright material: © Alamy/Barrie Rokeach p. **23**; © Corbis/Bettmann p. **22**; © Corbis/David Nicholls p. **5**; © Corbis/Frans Lanting p. **17**; © Corbis/J.Garcia/ photocuisine p. **30**; © Corbis/Lester Lefkowitz p. **24**; © Corbis/Ron Chapple p. **16**; © Corbis/Roy McMahon pp. **iii** (Contents, top), **7**; © istockphoto pp. iii (Contents, bottom), **32**; © Photodisc/StockTrek p. **4**; © Photolibrary Group pp. **8**, **10**, **12**, **13**, **15**, **34**; © Photolibrary Group/Pacific Stock p. **17**; © Photolibrary Group/Phototake Science p. **9**; © Science Photo Library p. **36**; © Science Photo Library/Andrew Lambert Photography p. **15**; © Science Photo Library/ Mehau Kulyk p. **19**; © Science Photo Library/NASA pp. **20**, **39**; © Science Photo Library/Raul Gonzalez Perez p. **10**; © Science Photo Library/Rod Planck p. **9**; © Shutterstock background images and design features throughout.

Cover photographs reproduced with permission of © Corbis/NASA/epa **main**; © Science Photo Library **inset**.

The publishers would like to thank literacy consultants Nancy Harris, Patti Suerth, and Monica Szalaj, and content consultant Dr. Ted Dolter for their assistance in the preparation of this book.

Every effort has been made to contact copyright holders of any material reproduced in this book. Any omissions will be rectified in subsequent printings if notice is given to the publisher.

Some words are shown in bold, **like this**. These words are explained in the glossary. You will find important information and definitions underlined and in bold, **<u>like this</u>**.

Contents

What causes this hair-raising experience? Find out on page 7!

Is toothpaste an acid or a base? Go to page 32 for the answer.

Matter in the Universe

Everything in the universe that we can see is made of matter. All objects contain matter and take up space. This includes you! Matter contains tiny particles, or parts that cannot be seen. These small particles are called **atoms**.

Inside an atom

An atom is made of tiny particles called electrons, protons, and neutrons. The center of an atom is called the **nucleus**. The nucleus contains moving protons and neutrons. Electrons circle the nucleus.

WOW!
A pinhead can contain 4 to 5 trillion hydrogen atoms!

Everything in our universe is made of matter.

Building blocks

Atoms are the building blocks of matter. Anything you see and feel contains atoms. Similar atoms can join together. Two hydrogen atoms can join together to make the gas hydrogen (H_2). Two different atoms can also combine together. Hydrogen and oxygen atoms can join to make water (H_2O).

TRY THIS!
Make an atom

Materials:

- 3 x 5 mm red pom-poms
- 3 x 5 mm blue pom-poms
- 4 white beads
- 2 pipe cleaners
- 150 mm (6 in) string, glue

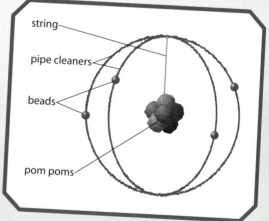

1. Make a ball containing 3 red pom-poms and 3 blue pom-poms. Place one end of the string in the ball's middle. Glue the string end and the pom-poms together to form a ball.

2. Push 2 beads onto each pipe cleaner. Connect each pipe cleaner to form a circle.

3. Place the pipe cleaner circles together. Tie on the pom-pom ball to hang in the center of the pipe cleaner circles.

4. Spread out the pipe cleaner circles to show the beads (electrons) orbiting the pom-pom ball (nucleus).

The red and blue pom-poms are protons and neutrons in the atom's nucleus. The beads are electrons orbiting the nucleus.

The Structure of an Atom

Each atom has a different number of electrons, neutrons, and protons. These small particles of atoms are called subatomic particles. Hydrogen is an atom. It has one electron, one proton, and no neutrons. Carbon is an atom, and it contains six electrons, six protons, and six neutrons.

This is a carbon atom. It has six electrons, six protons, and six neutrons.

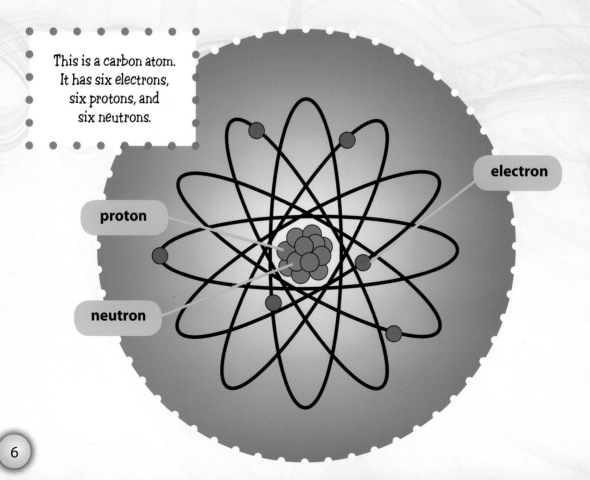

electron

proton

neutron

Positive and negative charges

Atoms like to have an equal number of protons and electrons. Electrons have a negative charge (-). Protons have a positive charge (+). They are opposite charges to each other. Neutrons are neutral, or have no charge. **When an atom has an equal number of protons and electrons, the atom has no charge and is balanced.**

TRY THIS!
Charged!

Materials:

- a balloon

1. Blow up a balloon. Tie off the balloon end.
2. Rub the balloon on your head.
3. Pull the balloon away slowly. Do you see your hair sticking out from your head?

Negative particles collect on the balloon. Your hair has a positive charge. So, the positively-charged hairs on your head are attracted to the negatively-charged balloon. Also, since your hair has a positive charge, it tries to repel itself. This is why it sticks out from your head.

How Atoms Join Together

Pick up an onion and peel each layer. An atom can be thought of like an onion. All the outside layers, or **shells**, contain the electrons. You have peeled away shells of electrons that surround the **nucleus**. Inside is the nucleus that contains the **protons** and **neutrons**. The **electrons** look like a fast moving, fuzzy ball around the nucleus.

Electron shells

When electron shells are full, atoms are balanced. If an electron is missing from the shell, atoms are **reactive**. Atoms will give away or take electrons from another atom. When two atoms share electrons, they can bond together to form something new.

Atoms have layers, like an onion. An atom's layers are called shells.

A water molecule contains one oxygen atom and two hydrogen atoms.

$$2H + O \rightarrow H_2O$$

How atoms combine

Atoms bond together when they are attracted to each other. Atoms will share or exchange electrons. If an electron is missing, the atom wants to fill this empty spot with another electron. When two or more atoms join together to make a **molecule**, they make different types of matter. Two nitrogen atoms can form a molecule of nitrogen gas (N_2). Three oxygen atoms make an ozone molecule (O_3).

Connecting the atoms

Molecules can be made from the same atoms. Molecules can also be made from different atoms connected together. Water is a molecule with two hydrogen atoms and one oxygen atom. It has the formula H_2O. Imagine dividing a water drop into smaller and smaller drops. Eventually, the water drop would be so small it could be divided into a single water molecule. Each molecule has two hydrogen atoms and one oxygen atom.

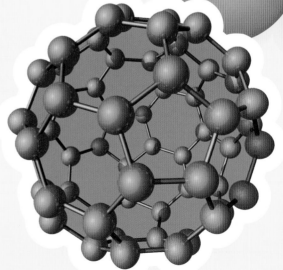

The buckyball molecule is made only from carbon atoms, joined together like this.

Did You Know?

Helium is a light gas. It contains two electrons and two protons. Because helium is lighter than air, balloons filled with helium float in the sky.

Ancient Egyptians knew that silk rubbed against an amber jewel created positive and negative charges.

Diamonds are completely made of carbon atoms.

One million hydrogen atoms would stretch across one grain of sand.

Quiz

1   What is matter?

2   What is an atom made of?

3   What are the three subatomic parts of an atom?

4   What two parts make up the nucleus of an atom?

5   What charge do protons have?

6   Where are electrons found in an atom?

7   What can atoms share?

8   What is a molecule?

9   What is water made from?

10   Can different atoms join together?

You can find the answers to this quiz on page 42.

Elements

An element is a substance that is made from only one type of atom. Elements cannot be split into a simpler material. If an element is broken down into smaller parts (**protons** or **neutrons**), it no longer retains the properties of that element. The simplest and most abundant element in the universe is hydrogen.

Pure silver is a soft, shiny metal. Sterling silver jewelry actually contains 92.5% silver and 7.5% copper. The copper makes silver sturdy for jewelry. Silver is also a good conductor of electricity and heat.

Structure of an element

Certain atoms have similar features. **<u>The number of protons in an atom determine the type of element.</u>** All atoms of an element have the same structure. For example, all atoms with two protons belong to the element helium. How do you make a new element? Add a proton to make a new type of atom.

Atomic numbers

Each element is identified by its **atomic number**. The atomic number is based on the number of protons in an element. Each element has an atomic weight, or **mass**. **<u>Atomic weight is the average weight of atoms that make up an element.</u>** The weight of the atom depends on the number of electrons, protons and neutrons. Add more electrons, protons and neutrons, and the element will have more mass. It will weigh more.

The metal lithium is lighter than water. Lithium can float on water and is so soft, it can be cut with a knife. It has a silver-white color. Lithium also reacts quickly with oxygen and water.

Properties of Elements

An element can have a **physical property** or a **chemical property**. Physical properties can be measured without changing the element. Examples of physical properties are color and the **melting point**. <u>**Chemical properties identify how elements react with other elements to change and make new material.**</u> Examples of chemical properties are how an element reacts with water or produces heat from burning.

Color

Some elements are named after a color. Rhodium salts have a pink color. Rhodium was named using the Greek word *rhodon* for rose. Chlorine is a yellow-green gas, and was named from the Greek word *khloros*, which means yellow-green. Some gas elements, such as oxygen, hydrogen, and nitrogen, have no color.

Conducting heat and electricity

Some elements are better at **conducting** heat than others. They warm up and cool down quickly. Metals such as iron and aluminum are good conductors of heat. That is why metals are used to make radiators and cooking pans. Nonmetals such as sulfur do not conduct heat well.

Metals are also good at conducting electricity. Gold, silver, aluminum, and copper are the best conductors. Copper and aluminum are used to make electricity cables. Nonmetals do not conduct electricity well.

Melting and boiling points

Elements can have different melting or **boiling points**. Physical changes occur when elements heat up or cool down. When a solid material melts into liquid, this occurs at a certain temperature called its melting point. An element's boiling point occurs when a liquid changes to a gas. And when elements cool down, they can reverse back from gases to liquids, and liquids into solids.

Many metal elements have high melting points. The metal magnesium has a melting point of 649° Celsius (1200° Fahrenheit). In comparison, oxygen has an extremely low melting point (-218° C or -360° F).

Reactivity

Some elements react with other elements very easily. A **chemical reaction** occurs when elements combine and change into products with properties. For example, oxygen in the air reacts very easily with iron to form iron oxide, which we know as rust. Phosphorus and magnesium are also very reactive. They burn easily.

Other elements do not react easily, because they are very stable. Gold does not react easily. It stays shiny, which is one reason people use it for making jewelry.

Phosphorus and magnesium are flammable, and very reactive. Magnesium is used in flares. Matches contain phosphorus.

States of matter

A **state of matter** is the form an element takes. A solid, liquid, or gas is a state of matter. Some elements can be found as solids, liquids, or gases. States of matter are a physical property, or feature. So how do elements become a solid, liquid, or gas?

In a solid, the atoms are close together, but they are still moving a little. When atoms are heated up, they move faster. As a liquid, the atoms move around freely and have no fixed shape. Heat up the atoms to a higher temperature and they spread out a lot more. In a gas, the atoms are far apart. Gases contain more space between the atoms, which move at very high speeds.

Gases

Some elements are found as gases. Hydrogen and helium are gases. They power the Sun. Oxygen and nitrogen make up 99 percent of the air we breathe. Most gases have no color.

atoms in gases

Liquids

Only two elements are liquid at room temperature. They are bromine and mercury. Bromine is a strong-smelling, reddish-brown element. Its name comes from the Latin word *bromos*, meaning "stench." Mercury is a silvery-white metal liquid. It is sometimes used in thermometers.

atoms in liquids

Solids

Solid elements can be flexible or hard materials. Copper and gold are flexible, metal elements. Copper pennies are zinc coins covered with a thin coating of copper. Silicon is a bluish-gray mineral and combined with oxygen forms sand or quartz. Solid iron has to be heated to high temperatures before it can be pounded into different shapes.

atoms in solids

TRY THIS!

Three states of matter

Can you observe three states of matter at one time?

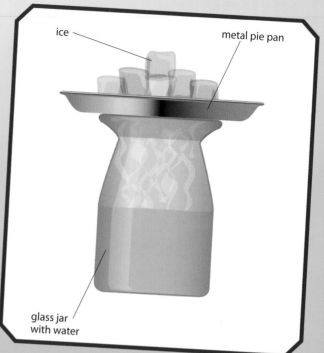

ice

metal pie pan

glass jar with water

Materials:

- a metal pie pan
- ice cubes
- hot water in a thermos
- a glass jar
- blue food coloring

What you do:

1. Fill a metal pie pan with ice cubes to become cold.

2. Ask an adult to pour the hot water into the glass jar. Observe the rising steam.

3. Add 3-4 drops of blue food coloring.

4. Cover the glass jar opening with the pie pan full of ice.

The hot water remains liquid. The steam rising inside the jar creates a gaseous cloud, and the ice remains frozen. There are three states of water at one time. The hot steam warms the pan to melt ice. As the steam hits the metal pan, it cools and condenses. The steam reforms into a liquid.

Water is interesting. At a special pressure and temperature, water can be found as a gas (steam), liquid, and a solid (ice) at one time. This is water's "triple point."

Did you know?

Plasma is called the fourth state of matter. Plasma is a mixture of positively and negatively charged particles. Plasma is a phase of matter that has enough energy for electrons to be separated from the nucleus. We actually see plasma in the sky, since our Sun is a big ball of plasma.

GOLD!

Ancient treasure

Over 3,000 years ago, artists crafted a solid gold mask to cover a dead king's face. Ancient gold treasure has been buried in caves, tombs and sunken ships. Dig up an ancient gold piece today and it would shine as if brand new. Yellow and shiny, gold does not tarnish.

Gold is one of the most precious metals on Earth. Gold's chemical symbol Au comes from the Latin word *aurum* meaning "shining dawn." Deep inside Earth, gold veins can be found with quartz rock and copper. Even seawater contains tiny bits of gold. The purity of gold is measured in carats. Pure gold is 24 carats.

WOW!

- Gold is a good conductor of electricity.
- Pure gold is 24 carats. Most jewelry is made with 18-carat gold, which contains 75% gold.
- Gold can be used for teeth fillings and lasts for many years.
- A special type of gold called Gold-198 helps doctors treat cancer.

Protective gold

Gold is very soft and can be pounded into thin sheets of metal. It resists corrosion, meaning it resists being destroyed or broken down by weathering. In space, gold reflects the Sun's damaging infrared radiation. Both spaceship panels and the visor of an astronaut's helmet are lined with gold. Gold can also be used to coat over or glaze glass windows. Gold reflects the Sun's rays to keep buildings cool in summer and warm in winter.

Thin sheets of gold protect the NASA space shuttles and astronauts.

Quiz

1 What is an element?

2 What is an element's atomic number based on?

3 How can an element's atomic mass change?

4 What is the most abundant element in the universe?

5 What is the smallest part of an element?

6 What is the main difference between elements?

7 How do elements combine?

8 What are the three common states of matter?

9 What is a melting point?

10 What is a chemical reaction?

You can find the answers to this quiz on page 42.

The Periodic Table
of Elements

In 1869 Professor Dmitri Mendeleyev was a Russian professor at the University of St. Petersburg. He was writing a chemistry textbook for his Russian students and did not have a good table that identified the elements. He decided to list the known natural elements on individual cards.

Building a table

Mendeleyev laid the element cards out as a table, and sorted them based on their properties. When he arranged the elements by their **atomic weight**, Mendeleyev noticed something very interesting. Based on an element's atomic weight, they had similar properties. He put the lightest elements to the left and heavier elements on the right. Each row below had heavier items than the ones on top. He also found that different groups of columns, or element families, had common chemical and physical properties.

Professor Mendeleyev

Missing elements

Mendeleyev was curious. By organizing the known elements by their atomic weight and properties, he found gaps in his chart and left them there. He believed these gaps were undiscovered elements. When new elements were discovered, they would fill the gaps. And Mendeleyev was right. One of Mendeleyev's predictions identified two missing elements in the atomic table rows that contained aluminum and silicon. In 1875 and 1886, scientists discovered gallium and germanium, two elements that closely met Mendeleyev's prediction.

Today, we call this table the **periodic table of elements**. There are a total of 118 elements listed on the periodic table. Of these, around 90 occur naturally on Earth and in the universe. The rest of the remaining elements were created by scientists in special laboratories.

Elements from Space

Iridium is a rare element on Earth, yet scientists found an ancient soil layer containing high amounts of iridium. Stony meteorites contain iridium. Some scientists believe Earth was hit by a huge meteorite 65 million years ago. This sudden impact may have caused earthquakes, huge storms, falling debris, and volcanic eruptions. All these factors may have killed off the dinosaurs.

Element groups

The periodic table of elements is a table that identifies all 118 known elements. Each element has its own chemical symbol in the table. You might recognize a lot of the most common elements. Carbon is C. Oxygen is O. Hydrogen, labeled H, is the lightest and first element.

Main groups

Scientists group elements in families based on similar properties, or features. Elements are organized based on their range of properties. Some elements want to share electrons. Other elements want to steal their neighbors' electrons.

In the periodic table, there are three main groups. The metals group contains metal elements. On the opposite side of the periodic table is the nonmetals group. Between these two groups lies the metalloids group, which have metallic and nonmetallic properties.

Turn to page 26. There is a full periodic table of elements.

Metal element fireworks burn a brilliant red because they contain the element Strontium.

TRY THIS!

Property of Metal

Are all metal objects magnetic?

Materials:

- strong magnet
- coins
- screws
- bolts
- nuts
- gold jewelry
- aluminum foil
- stainless steel pan
- paper
- pencil

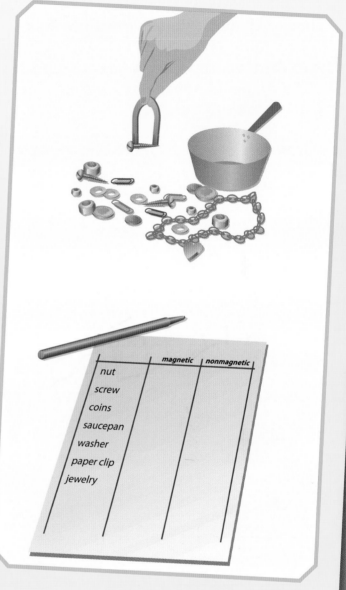

	magnetic	nonmagnetic
nut		
screw		
coins		
saucepan		
washer		
paper clip		
jewelry		

What you do:

1. Draw a table with three columns. In the left column list all the metal items. Label the remaining two columns magnetic and nonmagnetic.

2. Spread out the metal items on a table.

3. Hold the magnet close to each item.

4. Record your results on the table.

The periodic table of elements

As you can see, all the elements in the periodic table are represented by a chemical symbol. Aluminum (below, right) is Al. On the bottom right hand corner, the atomic mass of the element is listed. For aluminum, this number is 27. On the bottom left hand corner, the atomic number is given. (It is 13 for aluminum.) Read on to find out more about the groupings of the periodic table of elements.

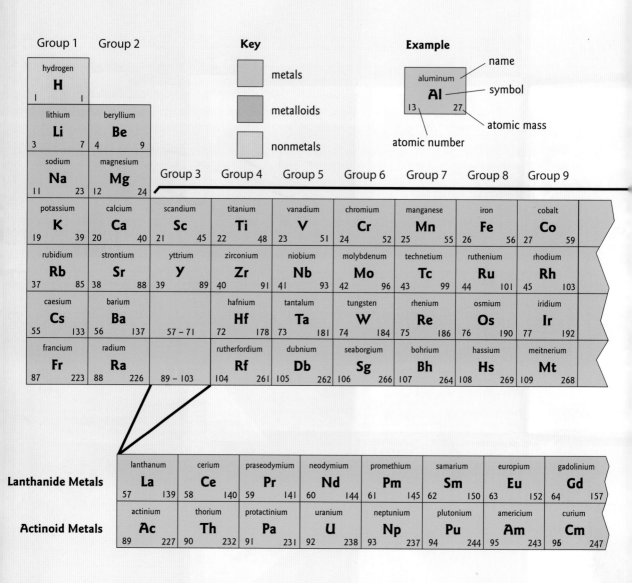

Groups and periods

The vertical columns of elements are called groups. The horizontal rows of elements are called periods. Some groups have special names.

Group 1: Alkali metals
Group 2: Alkaline earth metals
Group 3-12: Transition metals
Group 17: Halogens
Group 18: Noble gases

			Group 13	Group 14	Group 15	Group 16	Group 17	Group 18
								helium **He** 2 — 4
			boron **B** 5 — 11	carbon **C** 6 — 12	nitrogen **N** 7 — 14	oxygen **O** 8 — 16	fluorine **F** 9 — 19	neon **Ne** 10 — 20
Group 10	Group 11	Group 12	aluminum **Al** 13 — 27	silicon **Si** 14 — 28	phosphorus **P** 15 — 31	sulfur **S** 16 — 32	chlorine **Cl** 17 — 35	argon **Ar** 18 — 40
nickel **Ni** 28 — 59	copper **Cu** 29 — 64	zinc **Zn** 30 — 65	gallium **Ga** 31 — 70	germanium **Ge** 32 — 73	arsenic **As** 33 — 75	selenium **Se** 34 — 79	bromine **Br** 35 — 80	krypton **Kr** 36 — 84
palladium **Pd** 46 — 106	silver **Ag** 47 — 108	cadmium **Cd** 48 — 112	indium **In** 49 — 115	tin **Sn** 50 — 119	antimony **Sb** 51 — 122	tellurium **Te** 52 — 128	iodine **I** 53 — 127	xenon **Xe** 54 — 131
platinum **Pt** 78 — 195	gold **Au** 79 — 197	mercury **Hg** 80 — 201	thallium **Tl** 81 — 204	lead **Pb** 82 — 207	bismuth **Bi** 83 — 209	polonium **Po** 84 — 209	astatine **At** 85 — 210	radon **Rn** 86 — 222
ununnilium **Uun** 110 — 271	unununium **Uuu** 111 — 272	ununbium **Uub** 112 — 285	ununtrium **Uut** 113 — 284	ununquadium **Uuq** 114 — 289	ununpentium **Uup** 115 — 288	ununhexium **Uuh** 116 — 292	unuseptium **Uus** 117	ununoctium **Uuo** 118 — 294

terbium **Tb** 65 — 159	dysprosium **Dy** 66 — 163	holmium **Ho** 67 — 165	erbium **Er** 68 — 167	thulium **Tm** 69 — 169	ytterbium **Yb** 70 — 173	lutetium **Lu** 71 — 175
berkelium **Bk** 97 — 247	californium **Cf** 98 — 251	einsteinium **Es** 99 — 252	fermium **Fm** 100 — 257	mendelevium **Md** 101 — 258	nobelium **No** 102 — 259	lawrencium **Lr** 103 — 262

Creating Compounds

When atoms from different elements chemically react together, they form a new product called a **compound**. Compounds contain **molecules** made from different elements. <u>**Molecules in compounds have different properties from the elements that made the new product.**</u>

Salt is a compound, made of sodium and chlorine atoms. Sodium is a soft, silver and very reactive metal. Chlorine is a toxic, yellow-green gas. When these two different elements react, they form simple table salt crystals, or sodium chloride (NaCl). Salt crystals are white and dissolve in water. They are not toxic and are used often in cooking.

Na	+	Cl	$\rightarrow$	NaCl
sodium		chlorine		sodium chloride

Chemical formulas

Each compound has a chemical formula that identifies the number of atoms for each element. Table sugar is made from sucrose. One sucrose molecule contains 12 carbon, 22 hydrogen and 11 oxygen atoms. The chemical or molecular formula is written as $C_{12}H_{22}O_{11}$.

TRY THIS!
Gassing up balloons

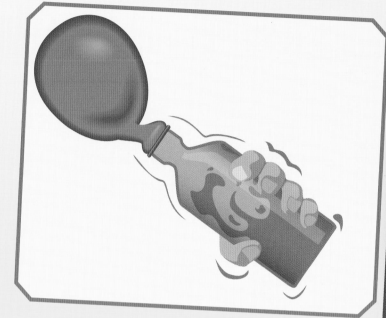

Materials:

- empty water bottle
- ½ teaspoon baking soda
- ¼ cup vinegar
- balloon

What you do:

1. Place the baking soda in the bottle.

2. Pour the vinegar into the bottle.

3. Quickly cover the bottle opening with the balloon.

4. Shake the bottle to mix the two materials together.

Vinegar chemically reacts with baking soda to make carbon dioxide gas, a salt (sodium acetate) and water.

$$CH_3CO_2H + NaHCO_3 \rightarrow NaC_2H_3O_2 + H_2O + CO_2$$

vinegar   baking soda   sodium acetate   water   carbon dioxide

When two different compounds mix, they form a new material with different properties. Baking soda contains sodium, carbon, oxygen, and hydrogen atoms. Vinegar contains hydrogen, carbon, and oxygen. What happens when they combine?

Connecting Atoms

Pour out sugar and salt into two separate piles. Both of these compounds are white, dry **crystal** grains. Salt and sugar dissolve in water and have no smell. Yet different elements join together to make salt and sugar. And they are connected by different **chemical bonds**.

Atomic bonds

<u>A chemical bond is a strong force that connects two or more atoms to make a molecule.</u> Elements like to be stable. If they need or have extra **electrons** to share, elements will give or take electrons to form different chemical bonds.

Ionic bonds

An **ionic bond** occurs when an atom either takes or gives away an electron to form a molecule. Sodium (Na) gives up an electron to chlorine (Cl) to make common salt (NaCl or sodium chloride). **Compounds** with ionic bonds have high melting points and can dissolve in water. They can **conduct** electricity when dissolved in a liquid.

$$Na \quad + \quad Cl \quad \rightarrow \quad Na^+ \quad + \quad Cl^- \quad or \quad NaCl$$

Sodium gives up its electron to chlorine to form NaCl.

Covalent bonds

A **covalent bond** occurs when atoms share electrons to form a molecule. Two hydrogen atoms share an electron to form a gas (H_2). Nylon (like the parachute in the photo) contains long chains of molecules connected by covalent bonds. Compounds with covalent bonds have low melting points and do not dissolve well in water. They do not conduct electricity very well.

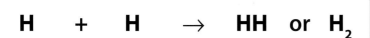

$$H + H \rightarrow HH \text{ or } H_2$$

Two hydrogen atoms will combine to share electrons and form a stable electron shell.

ACIDS AND BASES

Some **compounds** are **acids** or **bases**. These compounds have special properties that allow them to react with many other materials. When elements combine, they can have different types of chemical reactions. Understanding how **atoms** bond together can help chemists predict how other elements will react in the same family or group on the **periodic table**.

Acids or bases?

Common acids around your house include lemon juice, vinegar, and tannic acid in tea. Tartaric acid is in grapes. Acids can be strong enough to eat metal or weak like lemon juice. Hydrochloric acid in your stomach breaks down and digests food.

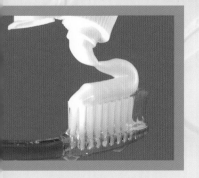

The opposite of acids are basic materials. Bases found at home include baking soda and toothpaste. Many bases are used to clean items. When an acid mixes with a base, the acid and base cancel each other out. The remaining product can include water, salts, and other chemicals.

What is pH?

Acids and bases can be strong or weak chemicals. Scientists identify whether a compound is an acid or base by measuring its **pH level**. Water has a neutral pH measurement of 7. Acids have a pH below 7. Bases have a pH above 7. The strongest acids have the lowest pH numbers (below 7), while the strongest bases have the highest pH numbers (above 7).

TRY THIS!

What gas is produced?

What happens when acids and bases react together? Can we identify the gas that is produced?

Materials:

- baking soda
- vinegar
- bubble mixture
- measuring cup
- medium sized bowl

What you do:

1. Pour 2 cups of baking soda in the bowl.

2. Pour 1 cup of vinegar over the baking soda. Notice the gas bubbles rising from the reaction.

3. Blow bubbles over the bubbling reaction. What do you notice?

Baking soda and vinegar produce carbon dioxide gas (CO_2).

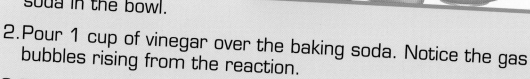

$$CH_3CO_2H + NaHCO_3 \rightarrow NaC_2H_3O_2 + H_2O + CO_2$$

vinegar   baking soda   sodium acetate   water   carbon dioxide

Carbon dioxide (CO_2) is heavier than air and sits above the reaction. The bubbles filled with air will float on the gas produced. We can see that it is carbon dioxide (CO_2) produced in this reaction.

MIXTURES

Not every material is an **element** or a **compound**. Some materials are **mixtures** of them. The elements and compounds do not react together. Each ingredient in the mixture retains its own properties.

Mixed up

The materials can be solids, liquids, or gases. Seawater is a mixture of sea salt, which is a solid, and water, which is a liquid. Sand and seashells are two solids that can be mixed together. Air is a mixture of gases.

Saltwater is a mixed solution of sea salt and water.

Suspensions and solutions

A **suspension** is a mixture where a solid material is carried by liquid. Sand rolling inside a wave is suspended, or held up in the seawater. The solid material can easily be separated from the liquid. If you let the suspension stand, the solid material will sink to the bottom.

A **solution** is a mixture where the materials dissolve. One material has to be a liquid. For example, sea salt mixed in water makes a solution of seawater. The salt dissolves in the water. The salt molecules do not react with the water molecules, but spread out in the water.

Separating mixtures

You can separate mixtures into what they were made from. By filtering the water, sand can be separated from water. You can use heat to evaporate water from seawater and leave the salt.

TRY THIS! Make your own volcano

Flowing lava is a mixture of molten rock and gases. Lava is molten rock and a mixture of minerals. Hot gases mix with lava inside Earth and can explode out of a volcano.

Materials:

- white vinegar
- baking soda
- alum powder
- unflavored gelatin
- red and yellow food coloring
- measuring cup

- flat metal pan
- newspaper
- measuring spoon
- 2 tall containers
- tape
- brown wrapping paper
- newspaper, tin foil

What you do:

1. Place the flat pan on paper laid out on a table. This demonstration can be messy.
2. In the pan, build a volcano with scrunched newspaper. Place the container in the middle.
3. Tape wrapping paper over scrunched newspaper around the tall container. Leave an opening, or crater.
4. Pour 1 tablespoon of baking soda into the container. Add 4 drops each of red and yellow food coloring.
5. Pour in $1/4$ cup of vinegar. Look out!

Now try this!

1. Place a new container inside the volcano.
2. Mix together 1 tablespoon each of baking soda, alum and gelatin. Pour the mixture into the container. Add food coloring.
3. Pour $1/4$ cup of vinegar into the container. How is this explosion different?

Elements of Life

Elements are the basic structure for the building blocks of life. About 99 percent of the human body is made up of oxygen, carbon, hydrogen, nitrogen, calcium, and phosphorus. These elements combine to make simple molecules such as water. They also make complicated ones the body needs, such as proteins.

Carbohydrates, proteins, and lipids

How do elements support life? Carbohydrates (bread, vegetables, and fruit) fuel our bodies. Carbohydrates contain mostly carbon, hydrogen, and oxygen. Proteins build muscle to support our body structure, or break up our food to release energy. Proteins use carbon, hydrogen, oxygen, nitrogen, sulfur, and phosphorus. Lipids are the body's fats and oils that are burned for energy. Lipids also insulate the body to protect from heat and cold. Lipids are made from carbon, hydrogen, and oxygen molecules.

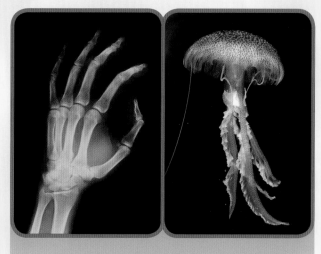

Calcium is necessary for bones. Without bone, our body would be like a jellyfish.

TRY THIS! Identifying elements

Can you identify elements you see and use every day? Copy this table and identify the main elements in these products. Add to this chart other common materials at home and school.

Materials:

- iodized salt
- baking soda
- glass container
- hydrogen peroxide
- toothpaste
- glass container
- silverware
- matches
- copper screws or nuts
- copied table of products and elements
- pencil
- on line computer

What you do:

1. Gather some of the common products listed above. Read the ingredients if listed.
2. If ingredients are not listed, go online and find information about the main elements in each product. (Ask an adult to help you.)
3. Write down the main elements you can identify in each product.
4. Write down other common products. What main elements do they contain?

COMMON ELEMENTS IN EVERYDAY LIFE

Product	Element	Element	Element	Element
Ammonia	Hydrogen	Nitrogen	Oxygen	
Baking Powder	Calcium	Phosphorus	Potassium	
Baking Soda				Carbon
Copper screw or nut				
Glass container				
Hydrogen Peroxide				
Matches				
Silverware				

Life on Mars?

Astrophysicists believe the Northern and Southern poles of Mars contain frozen caps of carbon dioxide gas (CO_2). These scientists have found evidence of water on Mars. If carbon dioxide and water existed on Mars, scientists believe life may have existed on Mars.

OUT OF THIS WORLD SCIENCE

Dr. Pamela Clark: Planetary geochemist

When Dr. Clark was 10 years old, she wanted to join the NASA Apollo missions to the Moon. In college, she studied geochemistry and geophysics. Planetary geochemists study the geology and chemistry of a planet's minerals and rocks. Dr. Clark is a planetary geochemist at the NASA Laboratory in Greenbelt, Maryland. She studies **extraterrestrial** physics. She focuses on rare lunar rocks and soils brought back from the Moon.

Identifying elements

Dr. Clark works with two special sensors called gamma ray and x-ray **spectrometers**. A spectrometer measures the wavelength radiation given off by materials, to identify their elements, age, and other features. Gamma rays and x-rays are high-energy radiation. The gamma ray and x-ray spectrometers help identify different elements on planets, moons, and asteroids.

ANTS Go Marching

Dr. Clark is working on a future space mission called ANTS (Autonomous NanoTechnology Swarm). Unmanned spacecraft will swarm and work together just like an ant colony. A new design of space rovers will be able to explore the surfaces of asteroids, the moon or distant planets. These rovers will be designed to land and can act like space scouts. Asteroids carry all the material when the solar system began 5 billion years ago. An ANTS rover could "bag and tag an asteroid," collect samples, and launch off to explore other asteroids.

One day, we may have a space base on the Moon. From there, Dr. Clark hopes to travel to Mars or Mercury.

An ANTS rover will be able to travel on asteroids and planets.

Quiz

1 What is the Periodic Table ?

2 What is the lightest element?

3 What is the chemical symbol for gold?

4 What is the atomic number and symbol for copper ?

5 What are the three main groups identified in the Periodic Table?

6 How is a molecule made?

7 What is a chemical compound?

8 How many atoms are in the chemical formula $C_6H_{12}O_6$?

9 Why do elements share electrons?

10 What is an ionic bond?

11 What is a covalent bond?

12 What are some common acids?

13 What are some common bases?

14 What is a mixture?

15 Why are elements important for life?

You can find the answers to this quiz on page 42.

Timeline

465 BCE	An ancient Greek philosopher Democritus discovered that there were tiny particles. He called the tiny particles *atoma*, which meant something to be divided. Today, we call them atoms.
100 CE	Alchemists began experimenting with metals to turn them into gold.
1869	The Russian scientist Dmitri Ivanovich Mendeleyev organized elements by their **atomic weight** on cards to establish the periodic table of elements.
1903 and 1911	Madame Marie Curie won two Nobel Prizes for her works in physics and chemistry. She helped discover the radioactive elements polonium and radium.
1937	Scientists started using cyclotrons to develop new elements. A cyclotron accelerates neutrons to extreme speeds to smash into atoms. Neutrons smashed into molybdenum created the element technetium (element 43).
1952	The radioactive element Einsteinium was discovered (element 99). Einsteinium was discovered when scientists examined tons of radioactive coral blasted by a nuclear bomb in the Pacific Ocean. It was named for the famous physicist Albert Einstein.
1969	The NASA Apollo 11 mission landed on the Moon. Armalcolite is named after the Apollo 11 astronauts (Armstrong, Aldrin, and Collins) This mineral was first discovered on the Moon. It has been found on Earth in the U.S. state of Montana and the countries of Greenland, Ukraine, and South Africa.
2006	A team of Russian and American scientists create the heaviest element ever seen in a laboratory—ununoctium. A cyclotron was used to bash atoms of calcium, which has 20 protons, into the element californium. The new element lasted only for 1,000th of a second, but suggested to scientists that other new elements could be discovered.

Quiz Answers

From Page 11

1. All matter is made up of atoms.
2. Electrons, protons, and neutrons
3. Electron, neutron, and proton
4. Protons and neutrons
5. Positive charge
6. Electrons are found in layers or shells surrounding the atom nucleus.
7. Electrons
8. A molecule is created when two or more atoms combine to make new matter.
9. Water is made from one oxygen and two hydrogen atoms.
10. Yes, different atoms can bond together.

From Page 21

1. Type of atom
2. The number of protons it has
3. By adding protons, neutrons, or electrons
4. Hydrogen
5. A subatomic particle
6. It is the number of protons. Add a proton and you create a new element.
7. Elements bond by sharing or taking electrons from other elements.
8. Gas, liquid, or solid form
9. When a solid material melts into liquid at a certain temperature
10. When two elements combine chemically, they form a new product.

From Page 40

1. It is an organized chart of the 118 elements.
2. Hydrogen
3. Au
4. Chemical symbol Cu, atomic number – 29
5. Metals, nonmetals, and metalloids.
6. Tightly connect two or more atoms together to make a molecule
7. A chemical compound is made up of atoms of two or more different elements that have reacted to create a new product.
8. 6 carbon atoms, 12 hydrogen atoms, 6 oxygen atoms
9. They like to be stable with full electron shells.
10. An ionic bond occurs when atoms combine to form molecules by either taking or giving away electrons.
11. A covalent bond occurs when atoms combine to form molecules by sharing electrons.
12. Lemon juice, vinegar, tannic acid in tea
13. Baking soda, soap, cleaning powders
14. A mixture is the combination of elements and compounds that are mixed together. These materials can be in the form of liquids, gases, or solids.
15. Elements are the building blocks of life. All living organisms have different elements that are used to break down food for energy, build living cells and structures, and allow life to exist.

The Properties of Elements and Compounds Review

◆ An **atom** is made of tiny particles called **electrons**, **protons**, and **neutrons**. Neutrons and protons are contained in the **nucleus**.

◆ When two or more atoms join together to make a **molecule**, they make different types of matter.

◆ An **element** is a substance that is made from only one type of atom.

◆ Each element is defined by its **atomic number.** The atomic number is based on the number of protons in an element.

◆ A **state of matter** is the form an element takes. A solid, liquid, or gas is a state of matter.

◆ The **periodic table of elements** lists the 118 known elements. There are three main groups in the table: metals, nonmetals, and metalloids.

◆ When atoms from different elements chemically react together, they form **compounds**.

◆ An **ionic bond** occurs when an atom either takes or gives away an electron to form a molecule.

◆ Some compounds are **acids**, and some are **bases**. Acids have a **pH level** below 7, and bases have a pH level above 7.

◆ A **mixture** is a material made of different substances mixed together, but not combined chemically.

Glossary

Acid A compound that releases a hydrogen ion in a chemical reaction

Astrophysicist A space scientist

Atom Smallest particle of an element that has the properties of that element

Atomic number The number of protons in the nucleus of an atom

Atomic weight The mass of an atom of an element

Base A compound that accepts a hydrogen ion in a chemical reaction

Boiling point The temperature at which a substance changes from a liquid to a gas

Chemical bonds The link between two atoms or molecules

Chemical property Properties that identify how elements react with other elements to change and make new material. One example is reactivity.

Chemical reaction The reaction that occurs when two chemicals react together to form new chemicals

Chemical symbol A single letter or two letters used to represent an element in chemical formulas and equations

Compound Product of two or more elements reacting together

Conduct To allow electricity or heat to pass through something easily

Covalent bond The bond formed by the sharing of a pair of electrons by two atoms

Crystal Type of material in which the atoms are arranged in an orderly pattern

Electron One of the very small, negatively charged particles that are a part of atoms, and are found outside the atom's nucleus

Element A pure substance that cannot be decomposed into simpler substances. About 118 elements are organized in the periodic table of elements.

Extraterrestrial Located outside of the Earth (somewhere in space)

Ionic bond The bond between two ions formed through the transfer of one or more electrons

Mass Amount of matter in something

Melting point The temperature at which a substance changes from a solid to a liquid

Mixture Material made of different substances mixed together, but not combined chemically

Molecule A unit of matter, formed when chemical bonds join two or more atoms together

Neutron One of the particles that makes up the nucleus of an atom

Nucleus Center of an atom; contains the protons and neutrons

Periodic table of elements A table that lists the known elements, organized according to the element's properties

pH level Level used to measure the strength of an acid or base, or the acidity of a solution

Physical property A characteristic of a substance, such as density or strength

Plasma Often called the fourth state of matter; it is a mixture of positive and negative charged particles. The Sun is a ball of plasma.

Reactive Tending to react to a stimulus. Elements that are reactive will combine with other elements more easily.

Shell The outside layer of something. The shell of an atom contains its electrons.

Solution Substance made when a solid, gas, or liquid dissolves in a liquid

Spectrometer A device that measures the wavelength radiation given off by materials in order to identify their elements

State of matter The form an element takes; can be solid, liquid, or gas

Subatomic particle Electrons, neutrons, and protons that make up an atom

Suspension A mixture where a solid material is carried by a liquid

Further Information

Books to read

Kjelle, Marylou Morano. *Mixtures and Compounds*. New York: Rosen Publishing, 2007.

Krebs, Robert E. *The History and Use of Our Earth's Chemical Elements: Reference Guide*. London: Greenwood Press, 2006.

Miller, Ron. *The Elements: What You Really Want To Know*. Minneapolis: Twenty-first Century Books. 2006.

Oxlade, Chris. *Elements and Compounds*. Chicago: Heinemann, 2007.

Pasachoff, Naomi. *Great Minds of Science: Neils Bohr*. Berkeley Heights, NJ: Enslow Publishers, 2003.

Scerri, Eric R. *The Periodic Table: Its Story and Its Significance*. Oxford: Oxford University Press, 2007.

Seddon, Tom. *Elements*. Strongsville, OH: Gareth Stevens, 2004.

Slade, Suzanne. *The Structure of Atoms*. New York: Rosen Publishing, 2007.

Solway, Andrew. *A History of Super Science: Atoms and Elements*. Chicago: Raintree, 2006.

Spilsbury, Louise, and Richard Spilsbury. *What Are Solids, Liquids, and Gases?* Berkeley Heights, NJ: Enslow Publishers, 2008.

Stwertka, Albert. *A Guide to the Elements: Second Edition*. Oxford: Oxford University Press, 2002.

Tocci, Salvatore. *Hydrogen and the Noble Gases*. Danbury, CT: Children's Press, 2004.

Ward, D.J. *Exploring Mars*. Minneapolis, MN: Lerner Publishing, 2007.

Websites

http://www.rsc.org/chemsoc/visualelements//pages/pertable_fla.htm
Go to this site and click on an element of the periodic table. You will have a truly "visual element" experience!

More Websites

http://www.eia.doe.gov/kids/energyfacts/science/periodictable.html
Find out more about the periodic table of elements and Mendeleyev at this colorful and informative site!

http://nasascience.nasa.gov/kids
NASA provides this site with lots of great links to science articles, activities, and more.

http://www.pbs.org/wgbh/aso/tryit/atom/
Build your own atom at this PBS-sponsored website!

Look It Up!

Do some more research on one or more of these topics:
• Carbon buckyball molecule
• Gold
• Life on Mars
• The periodic table of elements

Organizations

Office of Science
U.S. Department of Energy
1000 Independence Ave, SW
Washington, D.C. 20585
http://www.er.doe.gov/index.htm

Index